About Forgiveness:

"Forgiveness is the fragrance that the violet sheds on the heel that has crushed it." - Mark Twain

"The weak can never forgive. Forgiveness is the attribute of the strong." - Mahatma Gandhi

"Forgiveness does not change the past, but it does enlarge the future." - Paul Boese

"To forgive is to set a prisoner free and discover that the prisoner was you." - Lewis B. Smedes

"Forgiveness is not an occasional act, it is a constant attitude." - Martin Luther King Jr.

These quotes emphasize the transformative power of forgiveness and how it benefits both the one who forgives and the one who is forgiven.

Forgiveness Pledge:

This about me. This is personal. I can no longer keep silent and harbor ill feelings towards others. I can no longer hold on to hate, anger, sadness, resentment, regret, and guilt. I have to identify and evaluate those things that hinder me. I can no longer function in the alternate reality I created to comfort others or to comfort me. I choose to live in truth. My truth. And forgive those no matter what their intentions are/ were for me. Because on this earth only I have control over what is ahead of me. And I choose to pursue with a clear mind, a clean heart, and lead with forgiveness.

Sign here: _____

Date:_____

Step 1:     Accept & Dissect

We often tend to hold on to our personal hurt and resentment. There is not an effortless way to let go of hurt and mov on in a healthy way. When someone hurts or wrongs you, unbelievably the feeling of resentment is normal. Your feelings are valid. Acknowledging and accepting what occurred and how it honestly made you feel is the first step. It requires self-reflection. Focus on yourself and your emotions first. Once you come to terms with what happened and how it made you feel you can begin to heal from it. This takes a tremendous amount of honesty and transparency with yourself. We become so consumed at times at how others may view how we feel and how we react that we neglect ourselves and never fully accept our own feelings. Talking about, writing down, or even mapping your feelings out through art can help you work them out.

The next part of this step is dissecting.

Explore the other person's point of view for understanding, but not until you have accepted your own feelings. This does not mean that you must maintain a relationship or seek out an explanation for what they have done. Why not you ask? Chances are you may never receive a plausible explanation. At the very least you will never receive an explanation that will satisfy the hurt, pain, or discomfort they caused you. When someone hurts you, it effects the level of trust you have in them and others. Ask yourself, "Am I even going to believe them?" What you can do is 'put the shoe on the other foot." Explore the possibilities, but do not stay there. Remember, this process is for you; not them.


As we already stated, you must put yourself and your feelings first. Acknowledgement and gaining an understanding are the foundation and where the work begins. You are on your way!

Question: What method do you use to dissect how you feel? Talking to friends? Journaling? Praying? Exercise? Etc. How have those methods served you in the past?

Answer:

_____
_____
_____
_____
_____
_____
_____
_____
_____

Exercise 1:   Accept and Dissect

On the following pages, List what you consider the top 3 events that occurred over the course of your lifetime thus far that you have not yet forgiven.

Event 1

List 10 emotions you experienced during that time.

1. _____
2. _____
3. _____
4. _____
5. _____
6. _____
7. _____
8. _____
9. _____
10. _____

## Here & Now

This part of the exercise is designed to express how you feel RIGHT NOW. Write a brief description of current feelings below. And rate yourself at a 1, 5, or 10.

1-Happy     5-Indifferent     10-Hurt

Why?_____
_____
_____
_____
_____
_____
_____
_____
_____
_____
_____
_____
_____
_____

Event 2

List 10 emotions you experienced during that time.

11. _____
12. _____
13. _____
14. _____
15. _____
16. _____
17. _____
18. _____
19. _____
20. _____

## Here & Now

This part of the exercise is designed to express how you feel RIGHT NOW. Write a brief description of current feelings below. And rate yourself at a 1, 5, or 10.

1-Happy     5-Indifferent     10-Hurt

Why?_____

_____
_____
_____
_____
_____
_____
_____
_____
_____
_____
_____
_____
_____
_____

Event 3

List 10 emotions you experienced during that time.

21._____
22._____
23._____
24._____
25._____
26._____
27._____
28._____
29._____
30._____

## Here & Now

This part of the exercise is designed to express how you feel RIGHT NOW. Write a brief description of current feelings below. And rate yourself at a 1, 5, or 10.

1-Happy     5-Indifferent     10-Hurt

Why?_____
_____
_____
_____
_____
_____
_____
_____
_____
_____
_____
_____
_____

Step 2:    Take Your Time & Grow

There is no clock on forgiveness. I repeat, there is no clock on forgiveness. Sometimes we begin to pressure ourselves or begin to receive pressure from others to based on the relationship and/ or proximity to the person that us. Yes, there are times when that pressure comes from others because they want us to feel better about the situation and ourselves, but rushing your process by dismissing, deflecting, or discouraging someone's feelings can lead to prolonged hurt and stress. Forgiveness should never be rushed; especially not simply to accommodate others. The goal is to forgive fully and wholly. Give yourself all of time you need in the manner you need it. If you need time alone, take it. If you need to get out, go. If you need to seek professional help, book it! Every person is different and not everyone's process will be the same. Since our point of view's are strongly rooted in our individual experiences how we go about processing our feelings can vary. Just because a situation is similar does not mean your process will be a carbon copy of someone else's.

During this time there are three important questions to ask yourself. Why did this happen? Why did I think they were trustworthy? What can I do moving forward to avoid repeating these circumstances in the future? Once you have worked through your feelings of anger, sadness, resentment, guilt (or a combination of all four) learning from your past lapses in judgement make a stronger, better you. The confidence gained by knowing where tables turned will provide a level of confidence in the future when deciding who and what to allow in your life. Trust me, we all live and learn.

Exercise 2:   Time to Grow

Answer the 3 key questions in Step 2 for each one of the events that you listed in Exercise 1: Accept & Dissect. Take your time, be objective and honest. This is not about what they did. This is about you and your growth moving forward.

Event 1

How did this happen?

_____
_____
_____
_____
_____
_____

Why did I believe they were trustworthy?

_____
_____
_____
_____
_____
_____
_____

What can I do moving forward to avoid repeating these actions in the future?

_____
_____
_____
_____
_____
_____
_____

Event 2

How did this happen?

_____
_____
_____
_____
_____
_____

Why did I believe they were trustworthy?

_____
_____
_____
_____
_____
_____

What can I do moving forward to avoid repeating these actions in the future?

_____
_____
_____
_____
_____
_____
_____

Event 3

How did this happen?

_____
_____
_____
_____
_____

Why did I believe they were trustworthy?

_____
_____
_____
_____
_____
_____

What can I do moving forward to avoid repeating these actions in the future?

_____
_____
_____
_____
_____
_____
_____

## Here & Now

This part of the exercise is designed to express how you feel RIGHT NOW. Write a brief description of current feelings below. And rate yourself at a 1, 5, or 10.

1-Happy     5-Indifferent     10-Hurt

Why?_____

_____
_____
_____
_____
_____
_____
_____
_____
_____
_____
_____
_____
_____
_____

## Step 3: LET IT GO!!!

A prolific songwriter one wrote, "Sometimes you gotta lose to win again." To feel the full power of forgiveness you have to let go of any negative emotions attached to the wrongdoing. Anger, sadness, resentment, guilt, and everything in between, individually, and collectively can hold you back from living and experiencing life at it is fullest potential; at your fullest potential. Let all those feelings go!

Give yourself the opportunity to have a fresh start. You deserve it. You are not really "over it" until you can revisit the situation and the negative feelings no longer rule you. If you think back and are immediately triggered but cannot find your placement; repeat step 1. You have not made your peace. You have not accepted what happened. You have not provided yourself adequate time to grow or all of the above. If you have truly let it go speaking to, seeing and/ or mention of the person or thing that hurt you may not be a pleasant memory, but it will not shut you down and stir up those same negative feelings and physical responses. You are not truly ready to forgive until you do the work to become a better you. If you are there, proceed to Exercise 3!

Exercise 3:   Let it Go!

If you are not ready, write out your explanation for each event. Be as detailed as needed and revisit the previous steps with the details you have discovered. You have not failed! Remember it takes time and you are on your time!

Event 1. Why can't you forgive them/ it?

_____
_____
_____
_____
_____
_____
_____

Event 2. Why can't you forgive them/ it?

_____
_____
_____
_____
_____
_____
_____

Event 3. Why can't you forgive them/ it?

_____
_____
_____

## Here & Now

This part of the exercise is designed to express how you feel RIGHT NOW. Write a brief description of current feelings below. And rate yourself at a 1, 5, or 10.

1-Happy     5-Indifferent     10-Hurt

Why?_____

_____
_____
_____
_____
_____
_____
_____
_____
_____
_____
_____
_____
_____
_____

Step 4:     Forgive


The next, not last step to forgiveness is to forgive them. Sounds simple does not it. There is not set way to go about it. Just like with any process how you do it is based on you, your journey, your comfort level. One thing is for certain, your forgiveness can physically include the other person or not physically include the other person. That choice is up to you. But it needs to be a personal choice. You do not want to have any level of regret regarding how you chose to forgive. Do what is best for you and not anyone else; not the person you have forgiven, not others around you, do what is most comfortable for you.

For some it is enough to just forgive and move forward in their own mind, body and spirit and no longer allow what happened to be a headline in their story. Hey may share their revelation and journey with family and close friends, but it is so private to the point the person who committed the wrongdoing is never directly informed. It could lead to a happier life as you look forward to the future. Some others choose to include the other person physically through contact. That is an option, but not a requirement.

Step 3 was all about letting it go and during your process you may have decided to let that person go physically, mentally, emotionally, etc. Some feel that involving the person that hurt us is a testament of our growth and what we have learned in the process. Again, how you choose to go about it is strictly up to you. Whether it is by a private message through social media, text message, phone call or asking to meet in person (usually involving a family member, close friend, or romantic partner) most people only choose this option when reconciliation is possible. It is okay to forgive someone without granting them access to you, but if you want to reunite informing them of your decision is necessary. If you decided not to reconnect, but still want to let them know you forgive them, be clear. Let them know that you have forgiven then fully, what you have forgiven them for specifically but that you are not interested in bringing them back into your life. You are wondering why it is important to let them know reconciliation is not an option. It is important for you to set and stick to the boundaries you set for yourself. There is no guarantee that this person has changed or if they have that that change was for the better in your absence from them. As Tyler Perry says, "Forgiveness is for you. Not for them.

Exercise 4:   Forgive Them

For each event write out a forgiveness statement directly to that person or thing. Also, apologize to yourself. Everyone makes mistakes and have lapses in judgement. Make it personal.

*If you have decided to reconciliation is not an option:

Be sure to start this statement by letting them know that they are forgiven. State exactly why you are forgiving them. Read the statement aloud to yourself and then openly forgive yourself.

*If you have decided that reconciliation is an option:

Choose your mode of contacting them whether it be by social media, text message, phone call or in person. Pace yourself. Reach out to them to schedule a time that would be good for them to have a conversation. Remember there is no time limit on forgiveness. Reach out. Share your prepared

forgiveness statement with them and be sure to include any limits and boundaries you may have concerning reconciling. If over the duration of the conversation or in the days to come you see that reconciling may not have been the best option, let them know and let go.

Event 1

Forgiveness Statement:

_____
_____
_____
_____
_____
_____
_____
_____
_____
_____
_____
_____

Forgive Yourself:

_____
_____
_____
_____

Event 2

Forgiveness Statement:

_____
_____
_____
_____
_____
_____
_____
_____
_____
_____
_____
_____

Forgive Yourself:

_____
_____
_____
_____

Event 3

Forgiveness Statement:

_____
_____
_____
_____
_____
_____
_____
_____
_____
_____
_____
_____
_____

Forgive Yourself:

_____
_____
_____
_____

## Here & Now

This part of the exercise is designed to express how you feel RIGHT NOW. Write a brief description of current feelings below. And rate yourself at a 1, 5, or 10.

1-Happy     5-Indifferent     10-Hurt

Why?_____
_____
_____
_____
_____
_____
_____
_____
_____
_____
_____
_____
_____
_____
_____
_____

Conclusion: Keep Living

Continue to live your life with forgiveness. Whether someone cuts you off in traffic or steals your credit card forgiveness is one of the keys to personal growth. Holding on to unresolved, unhealed feelings can keep you in a time loop; never moving and never progressing. Not only does it stunt your emotional perspective on issues, but it also effects your development and decision-making. Adopting a lyfstyle of forgiveness sets you on a path to peace. There should not be anything looming in your lyf the does not bring you peace.

So, what is next?

Now that we have sorted through some passed occurrences feel free to use the following this guide in the future as needed. The following pages are a compilation of each exercise. Remember, talking about, writing down, or even mapping your feelings out through art can help you work them out.

Exercise 1:   Accept and Dissect

List 10 emotions you experienced during that time.

1. _____
2. _____
3. _____
4. _____
5. _____
6. _____
7. _____
8. _____
9. _____
10._____

Exercise 2:   Time to Grow

How did this happen?

_____
_____
_____
_____
_____
_____
_____

Why did I believe they were trustworthy?

_____
_____
_____
_____
_____
_____
_____

What can I do moving forward to avoid repeating these actions in the future?

_____
_____
_____
_____
_____
_____
_____

Exercise 3:   Let it Go!

If you are not ready, write out your explanation for each event. Be as detailed as needed and revisit the previous steps with the details you have discovered. You have not failed! Remember it takes time and you are on your time!

Why can't you forgive them/ it?

_____
_____
_____
_____
_____
_____
_____
_____
_____
_____
_____
_____
_____
_____

Exercise 4:   Forgive Them

For each event write out a forgiveness statement directly to that person or thing. Also, apologize to yourself. Everyone makes mistakes and have lapses in judgement. Make it personal.

*If you have decided to reconciliation is not an option:

Be sure to start this statement by letting them know that they are forgiven. State exactly why you are forgiving them. Read the statement aloud to yourself and then openly forgive yourself.

*If you have decided that reconciliation is an option:

Choose your mode of contacting them whether it be by social media, text message, phone call or in person. Pace yourself. Reach out to them to schedule a time that would be good for them to have a conversation. Remember there is no timeframe on forgiveness. Reach out. Share your prepared

forgiveness statement with them and be sure to include any limits and boundaries you may have concerning reconciliation. If over the duration of the conversation or in the days to come you see that reconciling may not have been the best option, let them know and let go.

Event 1

Forgiveness Statement:

_____
_____
_____
_____
_____
_____
_____
_____
_____
_____

_____
_____
_____


Forgive Yourself:

_____
_____
_____
_____
_____
_____
_____
_____
_____
_____
_____
_____
_____
_____
_____
_____
_____

Exercise 1:   Accept and Dissect

List 10 emotions you experienced during that time.

11._____
12._____
13._____
14._____
15._____
16._____
17._____
18._____
19._____
20._____

Exercise 2:   Time to Grow

How did this happen?

_____
_____
_____
_____
_____
_____
_____

Why did I believe they were trustworthy?

_____
_____
_____
_____
_____
_____
_____

What can I do moving forward to

avoid repeating these actions

in the future?

_____
_____
_____
_____
_____
_____

Exercise 3:   Let it Go!

If you are not ready, write out your explanation for each event. Be as detailed as needed and revisit the previous steps with the details you have discovered. You have not failed! Remember it takes time and you are on your time!

Why can't you forgive them/ it?

_____
_____
_____
_____
_____
_____
_____
_____
_____
_____
_____
_____
_____
_____

Exercise 4:   Forgive Them

For each event write out a forgiveness statement directly to that person or thing. Also, apologize to yourself. Everyone makes mistakes and have lapses in judgement. Make it personal.

*If you have decided to reconciliation is not an option:

Be sure to start this statement by letting them know that they are forgiven. State exactly why you are forgiving them. Read the statement aloud to yourself and then openly forgive yourself.

*If you have decided that reconciliation is an option:

Choose your mode of contacting them whether it be by social media, text message, phone call or in person. Pace yourself. Reach out to them to schedule a time that would be good for them to have a conversation. Remember there is no timeframe on forgiveness. Reach out. Share your prepared

forgiveness statement with them and be sure to include any limits and boundaries you may have concerning reconciling. If over the duration of the conversation or in the days to come you see that reconciling may not have been the best option, let them know and let go.

Event 1

Forgiveness Statement:

_____
_____
_____
_____
_____
_____
_____
_____
_____
_____

Forgive Yourself:

Exercise 1:    Accept and Dissect

List 10 emotions you experienced during that time.

21._____
22._____
23._____
24._____
25._____
26._____
27._____
28._____
29._____
30._____

Exercise 2:   Time to Grow

How did this happen?

_____
_____
_____
_____
_____
_____
_____

Why did I believe they were trustworthy?

_____
_____
_____
_____
_____
_____
_____

What can I do moving forward to avoid repeating these actions in the future?

_____
_____
_____
_____
_____
_____
_____

Exercise 3: Let it Go!

If you are not ready, write out your explanation for each event. Be as detailed as needed and revisit the previous steps with the details you have discovered. You have not failed! Remember it takes time and you are on your time!

Why can't you forgive them/ it?

_____
_____
_____
_____
_____
_____
_____
_____
_____
_____
_____
_____
_____
_____
_____

Exercise 4:   Forgive Them

For each event write out a forgiveness statement directly to that person or thing. Also, apologize to yourself. Everyone makes mistakes and have lapses in judgement. Make it personal.

*If you have decided to reconciliation is not an option:

Be sure to start this statement by letting them know that they are forgiven. State exactly why you are forgiving them. Read the statement aloud to yourself and then openly forgive yourself.

*If you have decided that reconciliation is an option:

Choose your mode of contacting them whether it be by social media, text message, phone call or in person. Pace yourself. Reach out to them to schedule a time that would be good for them to have a conversation. Remember there is no timeframe on forgiveness. Reach out. Share your prepared

forgiveness statement with them and be sure to include any limits and boundaries you may have concerning reconciling. If over the duration of the conversation or in the days to come you see that reconciling may not have been the best option, let them know and let go.

Event 1

Forgiveness Statement:

_____
_____
_____
_____
_____
_____
_____
_____
_____
_____

_____
_____
_____


Forgive Yourself:

_____
_____
_____
_____
_____
_____
_____
_____
_____
_____
_____
_____
_____
_____
_____

Exercise 1:   Accept and Dissect

List 10 emotions you experienced during that time.

31._____
32._____
33._____
34._____
35._____
36._____
37._____
38._____
39._____
40._____

Exercise 2:   Time to Grow

How did this happen?

_____
_____
_____
_____
_____
_____
_____

Why did I believe they were trustworthy?

_____
_____
_____
_____
_____
_____
_____

What can I do moving forward to avoid repeating these actions in the future?

_____
_____
_____
_____
_____
_____

Exercise 3:   Let it Go!

If you are not ready, write out your explanation for each event. Be as detailed as needed and revisit the previous steps with the details you have discovered. You have not failed! Remember it takes time and you are on your time!

Why can't you forgive them/ it?

_____
_____
_____
_____
_____
_____
_____
_____
_____
_____
_____
_____
_____

Exercise 4:   Forgive Them

For each event write out a forgiveness statement directly to that person or thing. Also, apologize to yourself. Everyone makes mistakes and have lapses in judgement. Make it personal.

*If you have decided to reconciliation is not an option:

Be sure to start this statement by letting them know that they are forgiven. State exactly why you are forgiving them. Read the statement aloud to yourself and then openly forgive yourself.

*If you have decided that reconciliation is an option:

Choose your mode of contacting them whether it be by social media, text message, phone call or in person. Pace yourself. Reach out to them to schedule a time that would be good for them to have a conversation. Remember there is no timeframe on forgiveness. Reach out. Share your prepared

forgiveness statement with them and be sure to include any limits and boundaries you may have concerning reconciling. If over the duration of the conversation or in the days to come you see that reconciling may not have been the best option, let them know and let go.

Event 1

Forgiveness Statement:

_____
_____
_____
_____
_____
_____
_____
_____
_____
_____

Forgive Yourself:

Exercise 1:   Accept and Dissect

List 10 emotions you experienced during that time.

41._____
42._____
43._____
44._____
45._____
46._____
47._____
48._____
49._____
50._____

Exercise 2:   Time to Grow

How did this happen?

_____
_____
_____
_____
_____
_____
_____

Why did I believe they were trustworthy?

_____
_____
_____
_____
_____
_____
_____

What can I do moving forward to avoid repeating these actions in the future?

_____
_____
_____
_____
_____
_____
_____

Exercise 3:   Let it Go!

If you are not ready, write out your explanation for each event. Be as detailed as needed and revisit the previous steps with the details you have discovered. You have not failed! Remember it takes time and you are on your time!

Why can't you forgive them/ it?

_____
_____
_____
_____
_____
_____
_____
_____
_____
_____
_____
_____
_____
_____

Exercise 4:   Forgive Them

For each event write out a forgiveness statement directly to that person or thing. Also, apologize to yourself. Everyone makes mistakes and have lapses in judgement. Make it personal.

*If you have decided to reconciliation is not an option:

Be sure to start this statement by letting them know that they are forgiven. State exactly why you are forgiving them. Read the statement aloud to yourself and then openly forgive yourself.

*If you have decided that reconciliation is an option:

Choose your mode of contacting them whether it be by social media, text message, phone call or in person. Pace yourself. Reach out to them to schedule a time that would be good for them to have a conversation. Remember there is no timeframe on forgiveness. Reach out. Share your prepared

forgiveness statement with them and be sure to include any limits and boundaries you may have concerning reconciling. If over the duration of the conversation or in the days to come you see that reconciling may not have been the best option, let them know and let go.

Event 1

Forgiveness Statement:

_____
_____
_____
_____
_____
_____
_____
_____
_____

Forgive Yourself:

Exercise 1:   Accept and Dissect

List 10 emotions you experienced during that time.

51._____
52._____
53._____
54._____
55._____
56._____
57._____
58._____
59._____
60._____

Exercise 2:   Time to Grow

How did this happen?

_____
_____
_____
_____
_____
_____
_____

Why did I believe they were trustworthy?

_____
_____
_____
_____
_____
_____
_____

What can I do moving forward to avoid repeating these actions in the future?

_____
_____
_____
_____
_____
_____
_____

Exercise 3:   Let it Go!

If you are not ready, write out your explanation for each event. Be as detailed as needed and revisit the previous steps with the details you have discovered. You have not failed! Remember it takes time and you are on your time!

Why can't you forgive them/ it?

_____
_____
_____
_____
_____
_____
_____
_____
_____
_____
_____
_____
_____
_____

Exercise 4:   Forgive Them

For each event write out a forgiveness statement directly to that person or thing. Also, apologize to yourself. Everyone makes mistakes and have lapses in judgement. Make it personal.

*If you have decided to reconciliation is not an option:

Be sure to start this statement by letting them know that they are forgiven. State exactly why you are forgiving them. Read the statement aloud to yourself and then openly forgive yourself.

*If you have decided that reconciliation is an option:

Choose your mode of contacting them whether it be by social media, text message, phone call or in person. Pace yourself. Reach out to them to schedule a time that would be good for them to have a conversation. Remember there is no timeframe on forgiveness. Reach out. Share your prepared

forgiveness statement with them and be sure to include any limits and boundaries you may have concerning reconciling. If over the duration of the conversation or in the days to come you see that reconciling may not have been the best option, let them know and let go.

Event 1

Forgiveness Statement:

_____
_____
_____
_____
_____
_____
_____
_____
_____
_____

_____
_____
_____


Forgive Yourself:

_____
_____
_____
_____
_____
_____
_____
_____
_____
_____
_____
_____
_____
_____
_____
_____

Exercise 1:   Accept and Dissect

List 10 emotions you experienced during that time.

61._____
62._____
63._____
64._____
65._____
66._____
67._____
68._____
69._____
70._____

Exercise 2:   Time to Grow

How did this happen?

_____
_____
_____
_____
_____
_____
_____

Why did I believe they were trustworthy?

_____
_____
_____
_____
_____
_____
_____

What can I do moving forward to avoid repeating these actions in the future?

_____
_____
_____
_____
_____
_____
_____

Exercise 3:   Let it Go!

If you are not ready, write out your explanation for each event. Be as detailed as needed and revisit the previous steps with the details you have discovered. You have not failed! Remember it takes time and you are on your time!

Why can't you forgive them/ it?

_____
_____
_____
_____
_____
_____
_____
_____
_____
_____
_____
_____
_____
_____

Exercise 4:   Forgive Them

For each event write out a forgiveness statement directly to that person or thing. Also, apologize to yourself. Everyone makes mistakes and have lapses in judgement. Make it personal.

*If you have decided to reconciliation is not an option:

Be sure to start this statement by letting them know that they are forgiven. State exactly why you are forgiving them. Read the statement aloud to yourself and then openly forgive yourself.

*If you have decided that reconciliation is an option:

Choose your mode of contacting them whether it be by social media, text message, phone call or in person. Pace yourself. Reach out to them to schedule a time that would be good for them to have a conversation. Remember there is no timeframe on forgiveness. Reach out. Share your prepared

forgiveness statement with them and be sure to include any limits and boundaries you may have concerning reconciling. If over the duration of the conversation or in the days to come you see that reconciling may not have been the best option, let them know and let go.

Event 1

Forgiveness Statement:

_____
_____
_____
_____
_____
_____
_____
_____
_____
_____

_____
_____
_____

Forgive Yourself:

_____
_____
_____
_____
_____
_____
_____
_____
_____
_____
_____
_____
_____
_____

## Exercise 1: Accept and Dissect

List 10 emotions you experienced during that time.

71._____
72._____
73._____
74._____
75._____
76._____
77._____
78._____
79._____
80._____

Exercise 2:   Time to Grow

How did this happen?

_____
_____
_____
_____
_____
_____
_____

Why did I believe they were trustworthy?

_____
_____
_____
_____
_____
_____
_____

What can I do moving forward to avoid repeating these actions in the future?

_____
_____
_____
_____
_____
_____
_____

Exercise 3:   Let it Go!

If you are not ready, write out your explanation for each event. Be as detailed as needed and revisit the previous steps with the details you have discovered. You have not failed! Remember it takes time and you are on your time!

Why can't you forgive them/ it?

_____
_____
_____
_____
_____
_____
_____
_____
_____
_____
_____
_____
_____

Exercise 4:   Forgive Them

For each event write out a forgiveness statement directly to that person or thing. Also, apologize to yourself. Everyone makes mistakes and have lapses in judgement. Make it personal.

*If you have decided to reconciliation is not an option:

Be sure to start this statement by letting them know that they are forgiven. State exactly why you are forgiving them. Read the statement aloud to yourself and then openly forgive yourself.

*If you have decided that reconciliation is an option:

Choose your mode of contacting them whether it be by social media, text message, phone call or in person. Pace yourself. Reach out to them to schedule a time that would be good for them to have a conversation. Remember there is no timeframe on forgiveness. Reach out. Share your prepared

forgiveness statement with them and be sure to include any limits and boundaries you may have concerning reconciling. If over the duration of the conversation or in the days to come you see that reconciling may not have been the best option, let them know and let go.

Event 1

Forgiveness Statement:

_____
_____
_____
_____
_____
_____
_____
_____
_____

_____
_____
_____


Forgive Yourself:

_____
_____
_____
_____
_____
_____
_____
_____
_____
_____
_____
_____
_____
_____
_____
_____

## Exercise 1:   Accept and Dissect

List 10 emotions you experienced during that time.

81._____
82._____
83._____
84._____
85._____
86._____
87._____
88._____
89._____
90._____

Exercise 2:   Time to Grow

How did this happen?

_____
_____
_____
_____
_____
_____

Why did I believe they were trustworthy?

_____
_____
_____
_____
_____
_____
_____

What can I do moving forward to avoid repeating these actions in the future?

_____
_____
_____
_____
_____
_____
_____

Exercise 3:   Let it Go!

If you are not ready, write out your explanation for each event. Be as detailed as needed and revisit the previous steps with the details you have discovered. You have not failed! Remember it takes time and you are on your time!

Why can't you forgive them/ it?

_____
_____
_____
_____
_____
_____
_____
_____
_____
_____
_____
_____

Exercise 4:   Forgive Them

For each event write out a forgiveness statement directly to that person or thing. Also, apologize to yourself. Everyone makes mistakes and have lapses in judgement. Make it personal.

*If you have decided to reconciliation is not an option:

Be sure to start this statement by letting them know that they are forgiven. State exactly why you are forgiving them. Read the statement aloud to yourself and then openly forgive yourself.

*If you have decided that reconciliation is an option:

Choose your mode of contacting them whether it be by social media, text message, phone call or in person. Pace yourself. Reach out to them to schedule a time that would be good for them to have a conversation. Remember there is no timeframe on forgiveness. Reach out. Share your prepared

forgiveness statement with them and be sure to include any limits and boundaries you may have concerning reconciling. If over the duration of the conversation or in the days to come you see that reconciling may not have been the best option, let them know and let go.

Event 1

Forgiveness Statement:

_____
_____
_____
_____
_____
_____
_____
_____
_____
_____

Forgive Yourself:

Exercise 1:   Accept and Dissect

List 10 emotions you experienced during that time.

91._____
92._____
93._____
94._____
95._____
96._____
97._____
98._____
99._____
100.    _____

Exercise 2:   Time to Grow

How did this happen?

_____
_____
_____
_____
_____
_____

Why did I believe they were trustworthy?

_____
_____
_____
_____
_____
_____

What can I do moving forward to avoid repeating these actions in the future?

_____
_____
_____
_____
_____
_____
_____

Exercise 3:   Let it Go!

If you are not ready, write out your explanation for each event. Be as detailed as needed and revisit the previous steps with the details you have discovered. You have not failed! Remember it takes time and you are on your time!

Why can't you forgive them/ it?

_____
_____
_____
_____
_____
_____
_____
_____
_____
_____
_____
_____
_____

Exercise 4:   Forgive Them

For each event write out a forgiveness statement directly to that person or thing. Also, apologize to yourself. Everyone makes mistakes and have lapses in judgement. Make it personal.

*If you have decided to reconciliation is not an option:

Be sure to start this statement by letting them know that they are forgiven. State exactly why you are forgiving them. Read the statement aloud to yourself and then openly forgive yourself.

*If you have decided that reconciliation is an option:

Choose your mode of contacting them whether it be by social media, text message, phone call or in person. Pace yourself. Reach out to them to schedule a time that would be good for them to have a conversation. Remember there is no timeframe on forgiveness. Reach out. Share your prepared

forgiveness statement with them and be sure to include any limits and boundaries you may have concerning reconciling. If over the duration of the conversation or in the days to come you see that reconciling may not have been the best option, let them know and let go.

Event 1

Forgiveness Statement:

_____
_____
_____
_____
_____
_____
_____
_____
_____

_____
_____
_____


Forgive Yourself:

_____
_____
_____
_____
_____
_____
_____
_____
_____
_____
_____
_____
_____
_____
_____
_____
_____

Exercise 1:   Accept and Dissect

List 10 emotions you experienced during that time.

101. _____
102. _____
103. _____
104. _____
105. _____
106. _____
107. _____
108. _____
109. _____
110. _____

Exercise 2:   Time to Grow

How did this happen?

_____
_____
_____
_____
_____
_____
_____

Why did I believe they were trustworthy?

_____
_____
_____
_____
_____
_____
_____

What can I do moving forward to avoid repeating these actions in the future?

_____
_____
_____
_____
_____
_____
_____

Exercise 3:   Let it Go!

If you are not ready, write out your explanation for each event. Be as detailed as needed and revisit the previous steps with the details you have discovered. You have not failed! Remember it takes time and you are on your time!

Why can't you forgive them/ it?

_____
_____
_____
_____
_____
_____
_____
_____
_____
_____
_____
_____
_____
_____

Exercise 4:   Forgive Them

For each event write out a forgiveness statement directly to that person or thing. Also, apologize to yourself. Everyone makes mistakes and have lapses in judgement. Make it personal.

*If you have decided to reconciliation is not an option:

Be sure to start this statement by letting them know that they are forgiven. State exactly why you are forgiving them. Read the statement aloud to yourself and then openly forgive yourself.

*If you have decided that reconciliation is an option:

Choose your mode of contacting them whether it be by social media, text message, phone call or in person. Pace yourself. Reach out to them to schedule a time that would be good for them to have a conversation. Remember there is no timeframe on forgiveness. Reach out. Share your prepared

forgiveness statement with them and be sure to include any limits and boundaries you may have concerning reconciling. If over the duration of the conversation or in the days to come you see that reconciling may not have been the best option, let them know and let go.

Event 1

Forgiveness Statement:

_____
_____
_____
_____
_____
_____
_____
_____
_____
_____

Forgive Yourself:

Made in the USA
Columbia, SC
13 August 2023